A ROOM IN THE TOWER

A Play in One Act

BY

HUGH STEWART

SAMUEL  FRENCH

LONDON
NEW YORK TORONTO SYDNEY HOLLYWOOD

Copyright © 1936 by Samuel French Ltd
All Rights Reserved

A ROOM IN THE TOWER is fully protected under the copyright laws of the British Commonwealth, including Canada, the United States of America, and all other countries of the Copyright Union. All rights, including professional and amateur stage productions, recitation, lecturing, public reading, motion picture, radio broadcasting, television and the rights of translation into foreign languages are strictly reserved.

ISBN 978-0-573-03301-8

www.samuelfrench.co.uk
www.samuelfrench.com

FOR AMATEUR PRODUCTION ENQUIRIES

UNITED KINGDOM AND WORLD
EXCLUDING NORTH AMERICA
plays@SamuelFrench-London.co.uk
020 7255 4302/01

Each title is subject to availability from Samuel French,

depending upon country of performance.

CAUTION: Professional and amateur producers are hereby warned that A ROOM IN THE TOWER is subject to a licensing fee. Publication of this play does not imply availability for performance. Both amateurs and professionals considering a production are strongly advised to apply to the appropriate agent before starting rehearsals, advertising, or booking a theatre. A licensing fee must be paid whether the title is presented for charity or gain and whether or not admission is charged.

The professional rights in this play are controlled by Samuel French Ltd, 52 Fitzroy Street, London, W1T 5JR

No one shall make any changes in this title for the purpose of production. No part of this book may be reproduced, stored in a retrieval system, or transmitted in any form, by any means, now known or yet to be invented, including mechanical, electronic, photocopying, recording, videotaping, or otherwise, without the prior written permission of the publisher. No one shall upload this title, or part of this title, to any social media websites.

The right of Hugh Stewart to be identified as author of this work has been asserted in accordance with Section 77 of the Copyright, Designs and Patents Act 1988.

CHARACTERS

(In order of their appearance)

MRS. TYLNEY.
LADY JANE GREY.
MRS. ELLEN.
MARY TUDOR.

SCENE.—A Room in The Tower of London. 1554.

Note.—The last sentence in this Play are the words actually used by the Lady Jane Grey.

A ROOM IN THE TOWER

SCENE.—*The* CURTAIN *rises slowly on a sombre prison room in a house on Tower Green.*
A high window at the back overlooks the site of the scaffold. L., *a door, and* R., *a door leading to an adjoining room. An oak table, writing-paper and books, etc. Plain oak chairs. We discover a grey-haired waiting-woman sitting by the table. She has a needle and thread in her hand and a silk garment on her lap, but she is not sewing, only looking straight before her, quite still. A young girl's voice startles her from her reverie.*

VOICE (*off*). Tylney!
TYLNEY. Madam.
VOICE. Is it time, Tylney?
TYLNEY (*aggrieved*). You've not been sleeping. . . .

(JANE GREY, *a prisoner in the Tower (with her husband, Guildford Dudley, both under sentence of death), appears in the doorway* R. *She is slight and small and her hands are constantly moving in quick nervous gestures. Her face is rather pale and drawn. Rather emotional, she is always simple and sincere.*)

JANE. I can't sleep. It's so cold in there. I have tried, but it's useless . . . useless.
TYLNEY. You look so tired.
JANE. I haven't slept for . . . it seems years.
TYLNEY. Have you looked in the mirror? Have you seen those dark circles under your eyes?
JANE. Mirrors don't tell the truth, they only show us masks. But what does it matter how I look? Few people will ever see me again. What time is it?
TYLNEY. It's still early, madam.
JANE. Whenever I sleep I dream.

TYLNEY. Of what, madam?

JANE. Of the place outside the window. I dream they are killing Guildford. I stand at the window and watch. It's horrible because I'm not with him ... I can't move!

TYLNEY. It is only a dream.

JANE (*by the window*). He looks up to me standing here, and when he sees me, he tries to smile so bravely. Then he takes off his ruff, and kneels down ...

TYLNEY (*leading her away*). Madam dear, you must put these thoughts from your mind.

JANE. Ah, if I could, Tylney ... if I could. Last night I dreamt I saw my father's head on a pike. It was lifted up and waved at me through that dreadful window. His mouth was open and the blood streamed down the staff.

TYLNEY. Your mind is distorted with all this trouble.

JANE. Why have they put me into this room? When they erected the scaffold the last time, the carpenters' hammer hit the nails into my brain. It was maddening, unceasing ... knock ... knock ... knock ... knock ... Is there any hope, Tylney?

TYLNEY. Of course there is; the Queen is very merciful and you are her cousin. Your youth alone ...

JANE. Youth! (*Laughs*.) You can speak about youth to me! In July I entered this palace as Queen; I was its mistress, the mistress of all England. And now ... what am I?

TYLNEY. We must forget the past now.

JANE. It's so difficult to forget; what is there to do here except to remember? (*With a great effort*.) Tell me, do they love their new Queen? There is some trouble, isn't there?

TYLNEY. It will prove serious, I'm afraid. She is so headstrong....

JANE (*cutting her short*). What is it?

TYLNEY. Well, it is feared that risings will break out throughout the country unless she will be ruled in time.

JANE. Ruled?

A ROOM IN THE TOWER. 7

TYLNEY. The people feel strongly against her proposed marriage.

JANE. It won't be my cousin who will give in.

TYLNEY. Parliament has presented a Petition against the Spanish marriage.

JANE. Parliament is so greedy. They expect us to sacrifice everything, our whole life's happiness, everything a woman treasures most, for what? For the country, for the sake of the people. What do they give up for their country? What are they willing, themselves, to sacrifice? (*By the window.*) Oh, Tylney, look! How beautiful it is, how beautiful those trees are below with the sun glimmering through the leaves. Like tiny green lamps . . . aren't they?

TYLNEY. Are they, madam? Those trees are very, very old.

JANE. I like them better from up here; you can't see their tortured, twisted roots.

TYLNEY (*brightly*). Shall I cut you a branch or two of leaves to-morrow? It would cheer the place up. I'll try to get you some flowers too; would you like that?

JANE. I'm sorry, what did you say?

TYLNEY. Would you like me to bring you some flowers, madam?

JANE. Oh, please.

TYLNEY. What flowers would you like?

JANE. I love every flower; they are all sweet. We have such a quiet garden at home. Lavender hedges and rosemary. Arbours loaded with red and yellow roses. I used to pick the tight, sweet-smelling buds and put them in my hair. There's a little pool I sat beside to watch my goldfish, they were so pretty . . . they used to nibble the crumbs from my finger-tips. I remember stealing there on warm evenings to listen to the nightingale. There are no nightingales here, no singing birds . . . only the croak of the raven, and they forbode evil!

TYLNEY. Come, madam, perhaps you won't be here very much longer.

JANE (*slowly*). Not very much longer!
TYLNEY. I mean, you may . . .
JANE (*unheeding*). They will come for me soon. Their footsteps will echo on those stairs . . . then someone will open the door and ask me if I am ready. (*Her hands creep to her throat.*) "I am quite ready, my Lords." They will lead me down . . . round . . . and round . . . and round the staircase . . . out into the air, and the light . . . everybody will gaze at me, perhaps some of them will feel a little sorry . . .
TYLNEY. Tell me more about your garden.
JANE. My garden?
TYLNEY. Yes, your garden at home.
JANE. Home? When my father told me that Edward had died, that I was Queen of England, I was frightened then. Terribly frightened. I believe I fainted.
TYLNEY. Poor dear.
JANE (*after a pause, sadly*). Sometimes I'm afraid that . . . that they only use me as a rung in the ladder. (*Breaking off.*) Oh, but what does it matter? What does anything matter any more? You don't know what my life has been, Tylney. My books were my only solace, my only friends. . . .
TYLNEY. But, madam, you are still very young.
JANE. What do you mean?
TYLNEY. They say the Queen has a forgiving nature.
JANE. I'm seventeen; is that young? I don't look young, do I?
TYLNEY. You are tired now. If you could only sleep.
JANE. Where is my husband? Why can't I see him again? I only want to touch him . . . to feel his arms round me, to be sure, to be sure that he wanted me. I must beg her, implore her to let me see him. Perhaps she will understand, and have compassion on us. O God, if she spares us . . . we may be free to-morrow, in a few hours! Guildford and I . . . we will go away into the country and forget, and begin life again, together. I think he loves me enough for that. (*She*

moves from the window.) Oh, Tylney, I don't understand. How strange a place the world is. I, who have never purposely hurt anyone in my life!

TYLNEY. You must put your trust in the Queen; she understands.

JANE. What?

TYLNEY. Your position, madam. How you have been used. How blameless you are.

JANE (*presses her hands to her forehead*). I don't know. Am I less to be blamed than Guildford, or Northumberland, or my father . . . or the Archbishop? (*A silence.*) Listen . . . Listen!

TYLNEY. Madam?

JANE. Did you hear?

TYLNEY. What is it, madam?

JANE. I thought I heard footsteps.

TYLNEY (*listening*). I hear nothing.

JANE. Someone is coming.

TYLNEY. I expect it's Mrs. Ellen. It can't mean that the Queen has arrived? And yet I told her . . .

(*The door L. opens quickly and* MRS. ELLEN, *a second attendant to* JANE, *comes in, closing it behind her. She is younger than* MRS. TYLNEY *and obviously excited.*)

ELLEN. The Queen is here, madam! She is being received at Traitor's Gate!

TYLNEY. Where is she?

ELLEN. She was mounting the steps beneath St. Thomas's Tower.

(*A roll of muffled drums is heard in the distance, and a herald of trumpets.* ELLEN *crosses to the window.*)

She will be on the Green at any moment.

JANE. Please, you will both stay with me? Don't leave me alone.

TYLNEY. No, no.

JANE. This means everything in the world, or . . .

TYLNEY (*interrupting*). Quickly, madam, there's your hair to be done.

JANE. Yes . . . my hair.

(*They both exit* R. ELLEN *remains at the window and keeps them acquainted through the open door with what is going on below.*)

ELLEN. She should have left the wharf now. . . . I expect she is passing under the gateway by the Hall Tower. Yes, I was right, here are her gentlemen, madam; they are walking by the row of beeches next to the wall which divides off her apartments. Now she has just entered through the arch leaning on my Lord's arm. He is telling her a joke, it seems; they are laughing a great deal. She is in fine humour, madam, God be praised; the Queen has a sour temper at times, I've heard. The gentlemen are waiting for her . . . she is joining them now, and . . . yes! They are coming across the grass, towards the Lieutenant's house. Oh, gracious! What high shoes she's wearing. She nearly fell then, if it hadn't been for my Lord's arm. (*She turns round.*) My heart's beating so I can hardly stand up myself. Are you ready, madam?

(JANE *enters, wearing a cap over her hair. She is still very pale, but she carries herself proudly.*)

JANE. I have decided to meet the Queen alone.

ELLEN. Very well, madam. You won't need me, then?

JANE (*smiling*). I won't need either of you. Return when the Queen has left.

ELLEN. Very well, madam.

(*She kisses* JANE'S *hand and exits door up* L.)

JANE. Tylney.

(TYLNEY *enters holding a diamond pendant.*)

TYLNEY. Coming, madam. Here is your diamond pendant. Let me put it on for you.

JANE. Do. I will feel Guildford is closer to me. He gave it to me.

TYLNEY. It's very pretty. (*She puts it on* JANE.)

JANE. Your fingers are trembling. Tylney, look at me. . . . Tell me, why tears?

A ROOM IN THE TOWER.

TYLNEY. You're so wonderful, my lady.
JANE. Am I?
TYLNEY. So calm.
JANE. I'm not frightened now, it's all gone suddenly. While you were arranging my hair I was praying, and God has heard me, and comforted me, that's all. Our fate is in His hands, I can't struggle against it; indeed, I must not. You must go now.
TYLNEY (*kissing her hand*). God bless you, madam!
JANE. God bless you!

(TYLNEY *exits* L. JANE *stands motionless. Voices are heard outside the door,* L.)

MARY (*without*). Leave us, gentlemen. We shall not be long here.

(*The door is opened for the* QUEEN, *and she stands for a moment on the threshold. Her lips are thin and downturned, but her eyes are not unkind and easily light up with enthusiasm, or anger.*)

Cousin Jane?
JANE. I am Jane Grey.
MARY (*after a pause*). You have changed.

(MARY *advances, carefully because of her high heels. The door is closed.*)

(*Considering her.*) The daughter of my Duke of Suffolk. ... I had not thought of my cousin like this. Quite beautiful, too! (*She laughs.*) It's strange, our family has rarely been famed for good looks before. You may sit. Which relative is it who has been so generous? Not your father, surely?
JANE. You are pleased to jest, madam.
MARY. Tush! No doubt those charms are responsible for your fame. We can see our Lords have acted wisely; what hope have I against such a creature? Men are so susceptible to fine features.
JANE (*protesting*). You are laughing at me. . . .
MARY. Troy was laid waste for Helen.
JANE. Have you no feeling?

MARY. Come, madam, I'm sorry to have to see you in such a place as this. You have been moved from the King's House?

JANE (*in a low voice*). Yes. Does that mean . . . that it will be soon now?

MARY. I know nothing about it.

JANE. This window directly overlooks the place. Is that so that I can . . . prepare myself?

MARY (*frowns*). I shall see that you are removed within a few days. Is that your wish?

JANE. It is my wish.

MARY. Very well, I shall instruct the Lieutenant. Were you happy in Leicestershire?

JANE. When I was learning; Doctor Aylmer was so patient and gentle. He made life seem so much more to me.

MARY. Your tutor?

JANE. Yes, madam.

MARY. We have heard of your great learning, Jane.

JANE. My father gave great care to my education.

MARY. Like my own, I think that is all I have to thank him for. He was very proud of my achievements. You speak in Latin, and Greek?

JANE. Oh, yes, I love them dearly.

MARY (*indicating the table*). What are these papers here?

JANE. Some Hebrew I have been studying.

MARY. Hebrew too! (*Examining the papers.*) Do you know the tongue?

JANE. I wish I knew it better.

MARY. I see you write in Arabic.

JANE. A little, madam.

MARY. My mother was my first teacher in Latin. When I was nine I replied in that tongue to the commissioners sent from Flanders. I can see the King now . . . how proud he was . . . (*She sighs.*) Have you repented, child?

JANE. Have I sinned, madam?

MARY. Why are you here?

JANE. Because of man's ambition.
MARY. You answer with a brief tongue.
JANE. Oh, madam, can you think it was my own desire so far to reach above myself? Indeed, I dared not of my own accord. Such a position held nothing but terror for me.
MARY. I can believe you.
JANE. All that I could ask from life . . .
MARY. What is that?
JANE. My husband's love, I think that is all.
MARY. A woman's life is one of sacrifice, and for such worthless men. You love Guildford Dudley?
JANE (*simply*). More than anyone in the world.
MARY. They say I should wed an English Lord and I say I will not. We shall see! There is not one I could care for; I know them too well. They are perverse, pig-headed fools! Yet you say you still love this . . . this man. The traitor who usurped our throne and set aside our Divine Right, as something of less importance than his own pride.
JANE. That fatal pride.
MARY. It is fatal to oppose God's will; people have discovered that and many more will discover it in the future. There are things which must be accomplished and which I will accomplish . . . alone if need be. It is necessary to proceed cautiously now, but they will be done before I die. (*She turns to* JANE.) Why did you plead guilty?
JANE. I am not very strong.
MARY. They dared to threaten you?
JANE. I was afraid, perhaps.
MARY. Was that all? Your father told you to plead guilty? Answer me!
JANE. Oh, madam . . .
MARY. Answer me!
JANE. I am guilty.
MARY. Do you know where your father is now?
JANE. What have you done to him?
MARY. Do you care?
JANE. He is dead?

MARY. He deserved to be hanged like a common footpad.
JANE. What have you done!
MARY. I cannot understand you, Jane. He is not worth a moment's anxiety. That is why I have spared him. He is such a fool; I think he has been frightened enough.
JANE. You have spared my father?
MARY. He was shown the dungeons, and he has seen a man on the rack. I would not stain my shoe to crush a worm under foot.
JANE (*on her knees*). Oh, God bless you! God bless you! Your mercy will be rewarded. (*Her voice faltering.*) Madam, there is something . . .
MARY. Well?
JANE. If you think me bold, I am only made so by your exceeding goodness. It urges me to hope, to believe that you will extend your compassion to . . . to the Archbishop Cranmer . . . (*The* QUEEN *starts.*) Oh, cousin, I beseech you to spare the old man.
MARY. I must have no heart.
JANE. But you are not heartless, you are not. You have shown me how great it is.
MARY (*touched*). You are the first person to say that to me.
JANE. The Primate is old . . .
MARY. He is a traitor like the rest of you!
JANE. No, madam, he is not in entire possession of his strength. When he consented to my succession it was only after a long period in which he opposed it. He has given many years in devoted allegiance to the Crown. Oh, cousin, don't dishonour him in his old age; he was worn down, he feared for his life. . . . don't let them kill him!
MARY. They cannot, without my consent.
JANE. Then have mercy on him; let his gratitude be added to mine, I implore you.
MARY. I shall see no hurt comes to him; that is all I can promise now.
JANE. You promise that?

(MARY *nods*.)

But you are the Sovereign.

MARY (*sadly*). I am only a woman, Jane. Ah, if I had been a man . . . everything would be so easy. I should command and dictate and make England glorious. I should throw off this heavy cloak of hypocrisy. I should be a slave to no living person, only to God.

JANE (*softly*). Your people believe in you.

MARY. Do they? Do you think they do?

JANE. Yes.

MARY. But they don't understand. I am not a hard woman, and God knows my life has been hard. I must do these things if it breaks my heart. To restore our violated faith and unite, with bonds of steel, the two greatest countries in the world. That is my mission, and I have no wish to die with the certainty it has failed. (*To* JANE.) In a few days you will leave this prison-house, for ever.

JANE (*quietly, after a pause*). I don't think I can die, as I ought to die, unless I see him again.

MARY. Your husband?

JANE. Yes. You see my life has been so empty; if there is no life after death . . . nothing, no afterwards . . . I . . . I couldn't bear it! It's all that I have left . . . that I will be with him in heaven.

MARY. My poor child, you need not be afraid.

JANE. I'm not really afraid, only . . . sometimes . . .

MARY. I mean you to go into life, not death.

JANE (*in a whisper*). Life!

MARY. I pardon you, Jane.

JANE. Into life! Both of us!

MARY. I am satisfied of your innocence.

JANE. Both of us?

MARY (*evading the question*). There is life waiting for you, full of sunshine, and joy, beautiful things . . . and children.

JANE. Oh, madam . . . madam! (*With shaking hands she raises the hem of the* QUEEN'S *skirt to her lips.*)

My happiness . . . I can't express it. I feel . . . it's so great . . . it won't let me speak.

MARY (*tenderly*). I understand. There is no cause for you to kneel.

JANE. We shall pray for you and bless you . . . in every prayer of our lives.

MARY. Remember me, when you are happy, will you?

JANE. Always.

MARY. I shall need all your prayers. It is hard . . . it is so hard sometimes, to do my duty. I wish I were finished with it all, but I must go onwards. (*She rises.*) Duty comes before everything. Everything. I must leave you. I have been too long already.

JANE. Must you . . . must you go?

MARY (*nods*). Duty compels me; it has been like that, always. Farewell.

(*She moves away, and turns for a moment at the door.*)
Be wise, Jane. (*Off stage.*) Your arm, my Lord, please. I tire so quickly now.

(*The door closes.* JANE *remains on her knees crying quietly for several minutes. When she rises she walks across to the window. The roll of drums is heard again.* TYLNEY *comes in,* L. *She has just heard some fateful message, which she does not know, at first, how to impart to her mistress.*)

JANE (*without looking up*). Is that you, Tylney?

TYLNEY. Yes, madam.

JANE. Dear Tylney . . . you have been so kind to me. So few people have been kind in my life. (*She takes her hands.*) Why do you look so pale? And . . . yes, there are still tears in your eyes.

TYLNEY (*in a strained voice*). The Queen . . .

JANE. You do care for me, don't you?

TYLNEY. Oh, madam, very greatly.

JANE. Then why are there tears?

TYLNEY. She has pardoned you? I knew.

JANE. Both of us! I can't believe it yet. I can't

A ROOM IN THE TOWER.

believe it. I'm not sure . . . that I'm not asleep really. It may only be a dream.

TYLNEY. Perhaps you are . . . asleep.

JANE. If I am dreaming, don't wake me. Please don't wake me. (*With her arms around* TYLNEY'S *neck.*) Oh, Tylney, we are free . . . free, don't you understand? I won't be here any more. I don't like this room, it's full of ghosts.

TYLNEY. Madam, listen . . .

JANE (*in ecstasy*). She said in a few days, only a few days more. How can I live till then? Guildford, Guildford, I wish I were with you now. Don't you realize what this means? It means life together . . . it means we can walk under the sky, and hear the birds again; it means you.

TYLNEY (*anguished*). Oh, madam, don't! I have something I must tell you at once.

(JANE *turns slowly.*)

JANE. Tylney, what is the matter with you? What are you saying?

TYLNEY. Oh, my dear lady . . . the news has just been brought.

JANE (*in sudden terror*). My God! What is it? What is it?

TYLNEY. Your father has joined the conspirators!

JANE. My father . . .

TYLNEY. Against Her Majesty. He and Sir Thomas Wyatt have occupied Rochester with their men. They have issued a proclamation . . . against the Queen's marriage.

JANE (*after a long pause*). It's not true. It's not true! It's a false report. . . . He couldn't! I won't believe it!

TYLNEY. God forgive them, it is the truth. I heard it from the messenger myself.

JANE. He was lying!

TYLNEY. I fear . . .

JANE (*almost voiceless*). God wouldn't do this to me?

TYLNEY. Everywhere they are rising against her,

and joining Sir Thomas. They say he will march on London. It's revolution!

JANE. Revolution!

TYLNEY. We thought you should be told, now.

JANE (*her voice breaking*). Yes . . . yes, that was right. But what have I done? What have I done to deserve this? Does she know . . . did she know?

TYLNEY (*shakes her head*). Not yet.

(JANE *has gone very white; she realizes this move has sealed her fate. The roll of drums is heard again, very faintly.* TYLNEY *bursts into tears.*)

JANE. Then this is the end. . . . I think it was too wonderful to be true. I was born to suffer, but . . . this is hurting so.

(*The drums are heard more loudly. She suddenly puts her arms around* TYLNEY'S *shoulders.*)

Oh, no, Tylney . . . you mustn't cry, you mustn't cry, for my sake. Look! Such a beautiful sunset . . . there must be a God to create that. Death holds no terror for me now, I know life won't end with the grave, in darkness. There is a great glory shining behind the clouds. . . . I feel no pain . . . my Spirit will spring rejoicing into the Eternal Light, where I hope the mercy of God will receive it.

CURTAIN.

www.ingramcontent.com/pod-product-compliance
Ingram Content Group UK Ltd.
Pitfield, Milton Keynes, MK11 3LW, UK
UKHW021837210426
5322IPUK00021B/332